GU0095090

Maxine's
GUIDE TO
AGING
GRACELESSLY

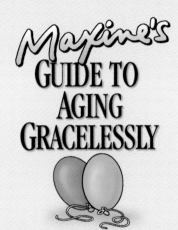

For information, write Andrews McMeel Publishing, an
Andrews McMeel Universal company, 4520 Main Street,
Kansas City, Missouri 64111.

www.andrewsmcmeel.com
www.shoebox.com

ISBN: 0-7407-0082-0

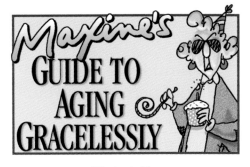

Maxine's
GUIDE TO
AGING
GRACELESSLY

Illustrated by
John Wagner

Written by
Chris Brethwaite, Bill Bridgeman, Bill Gray,
Allyson Jones, Kevin Kinzer, Mark Oatman,
Dee Ann Stewart, and Dan Taylor

Book design by
Terry O'Reagan

Birthdays can put
a lot of pressure on you.

They're like the 64-ounce
soda that seemed like a
good idea at the beginning
of the trip.

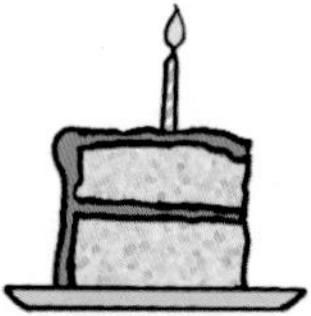

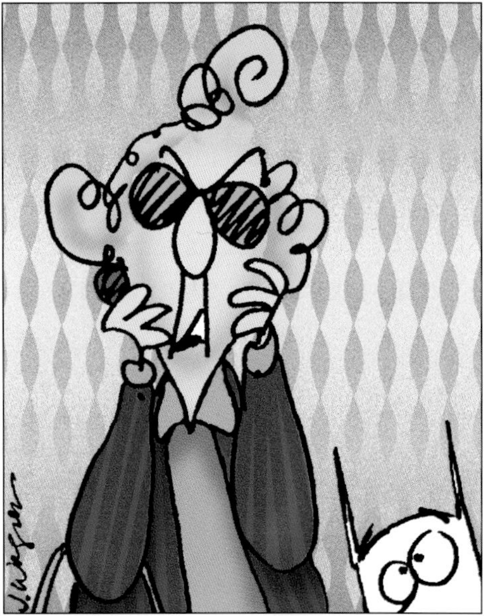
J. Wagner

Don't you just hate it
when somebody gives you
a birthday gift as cheap as
the one you gave them
last year?

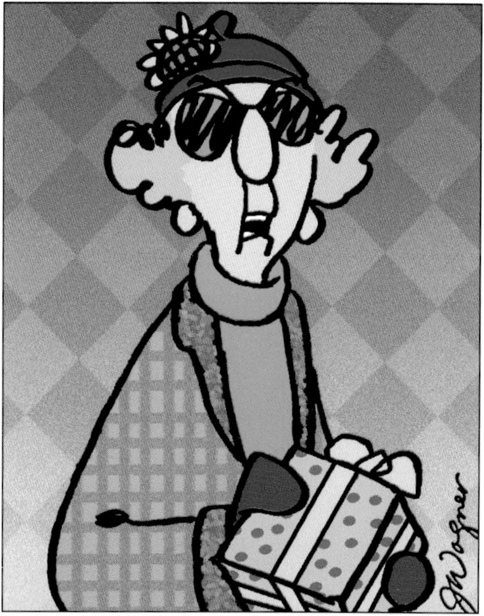
JWagner

Birthdays and friends
go together
like breathing
and complaining.

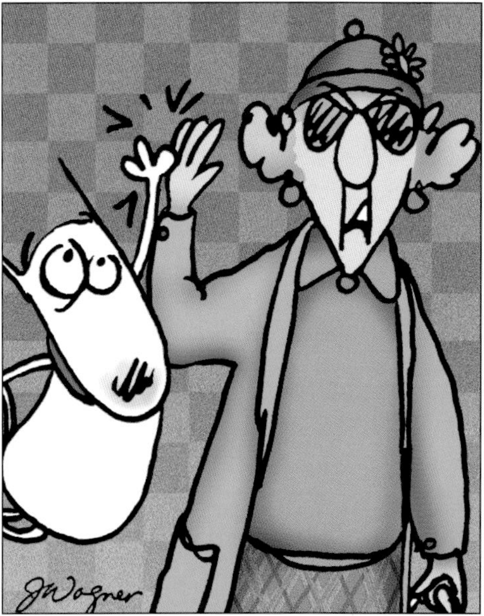

JWagner

Did you hear about
the new Birthday Diet?

It's called
"Eat Whatever the Heck
You Want."

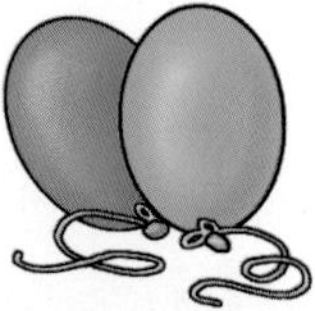

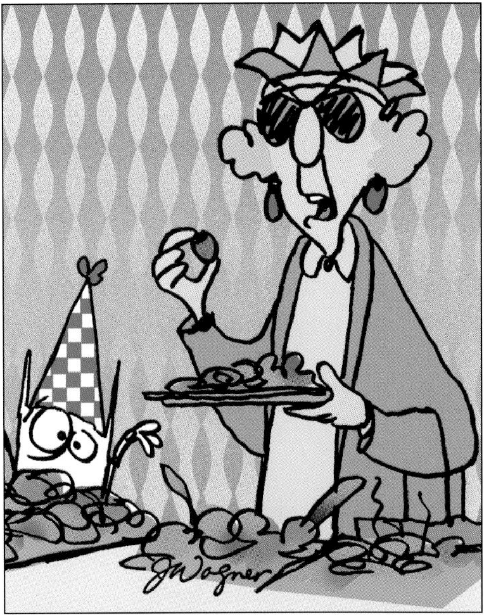
JWagner

The only time
I use the phrase
"Oldie but Goodie"
is when I decide
to eat yogurt past
its expiration date.

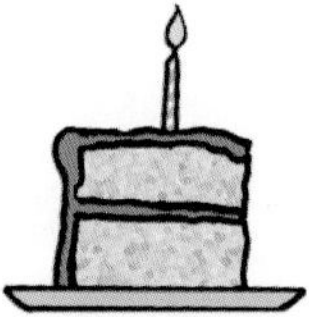

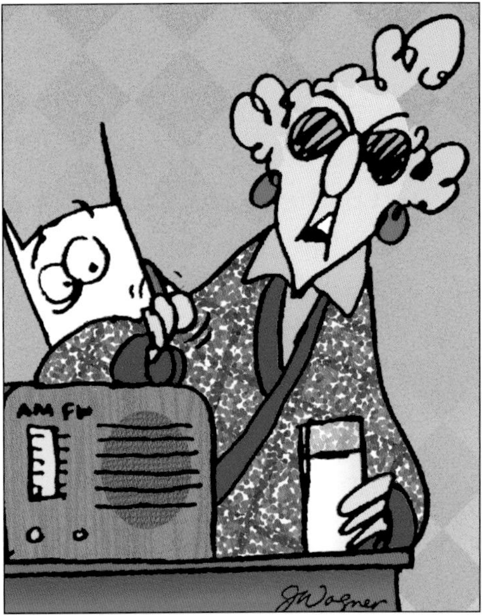
AM FM
JWagner

When people say you're
"aging like a fine wine"
what they really mean
is that most of the
contents have settled
to the bottom.

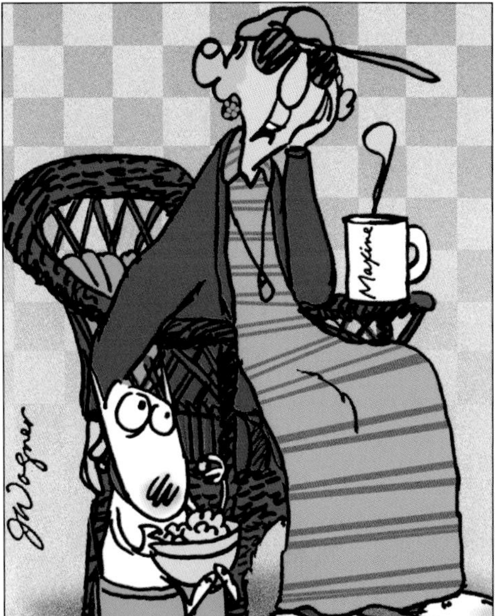
Maxine

You know you're
getting older when
you go to moon
somebody, and a cow
tries to jump over
your butt.

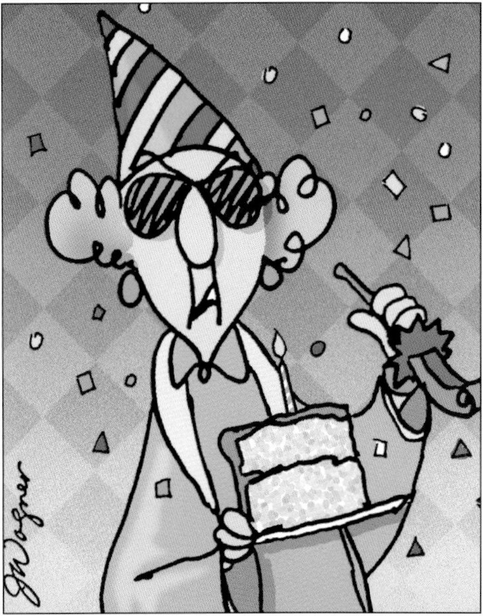

Another birthday?

Well, whoop-de-droop.

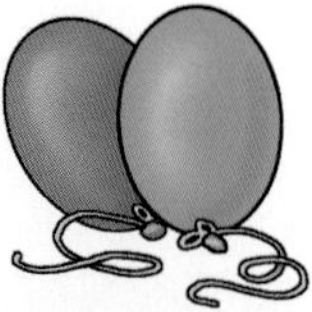

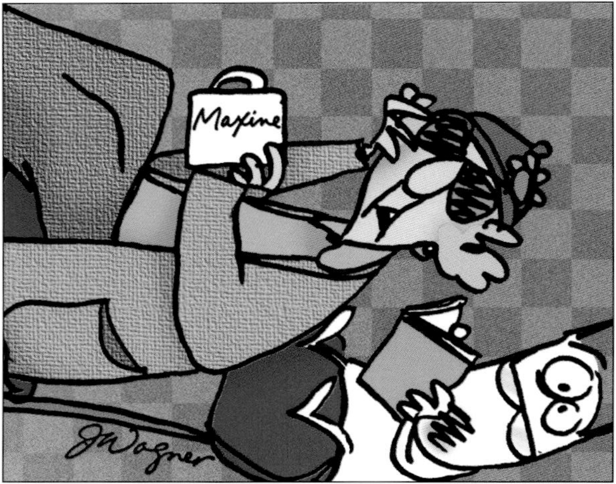
Maxine
JWagner

Who's the cone-headed dimwit who designed the birthday party hat, anyway?

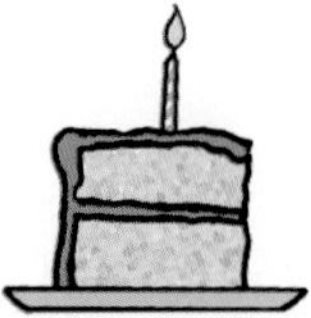

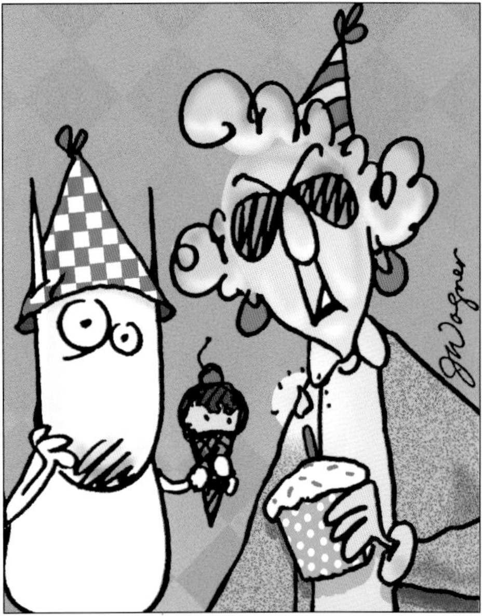
JWagner

With age comes wisdom.
With wisdom comes respect.

And with the senior meal
comes two biscuits and
bottomless decaf
for $1.99.

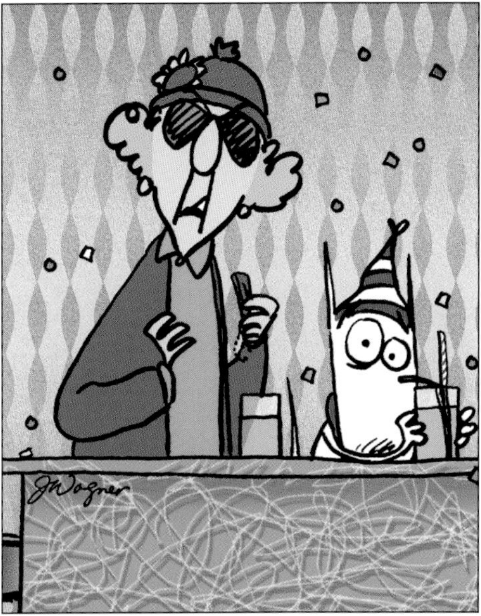
JWagner

A birthday is
a good time to party
till the cows come home.

Then make hamburgers.
Maybe a jacket.

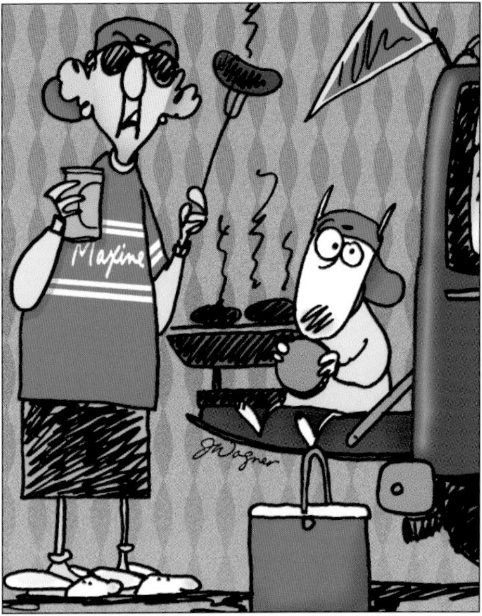
Maxine
JWagner

Thought of a new fun birthday party game.

It's called "Go Home."

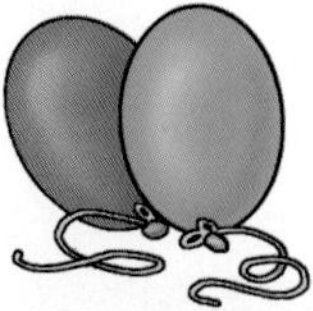

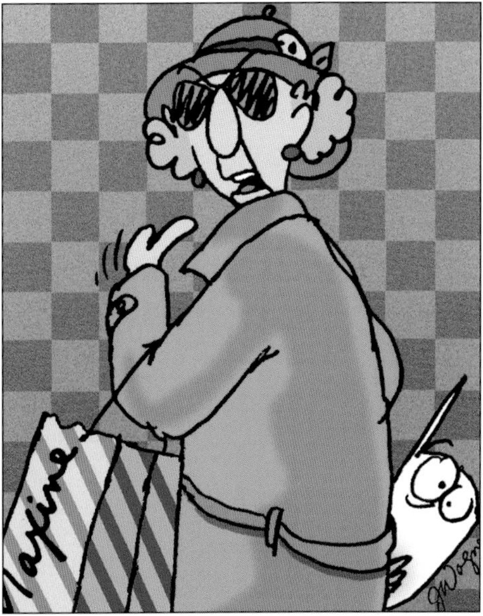

Birthdays are like
relatives at the holidays.

They show up whether
you want 'em to or not.

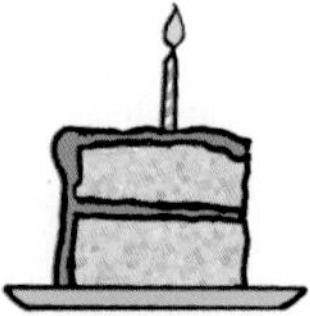

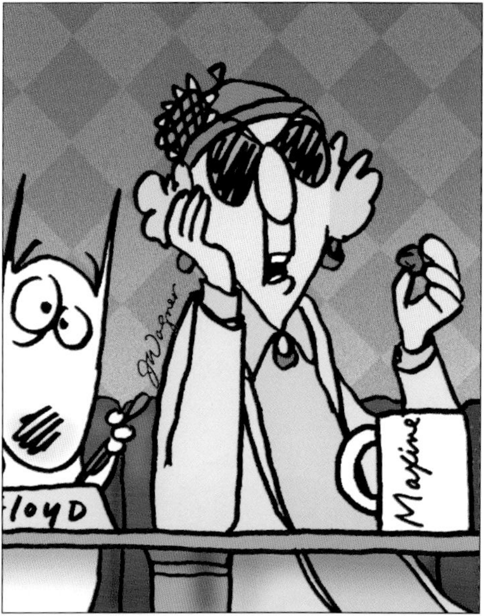

Maxine

A birthday reminder:
Smile and the world
smiles with you.

Unless you've
forgotten to put
in your teeth.

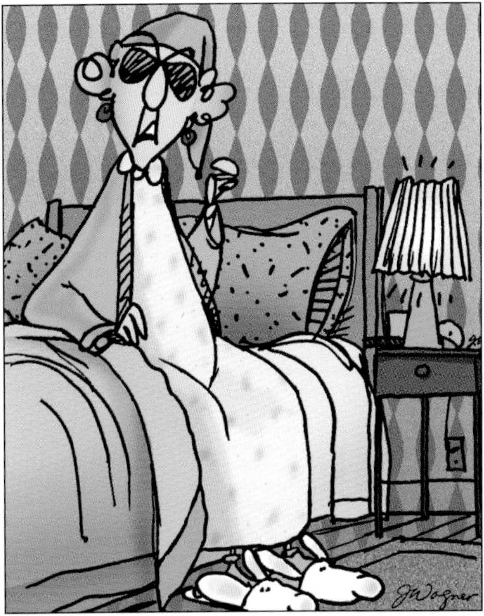
JWagner

I never get the
one thing I always
want for my birthday...

left alone.

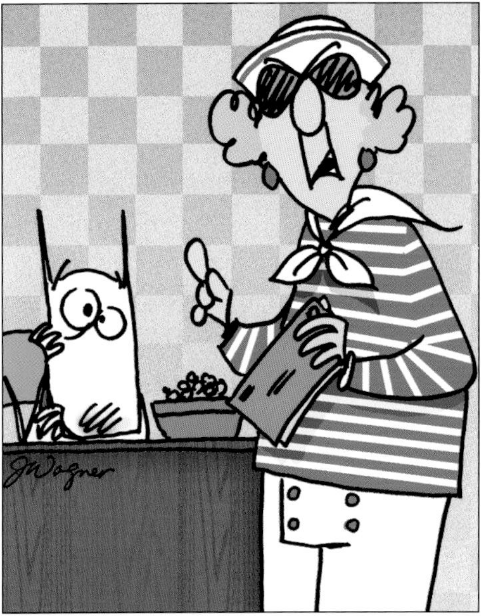
JWagner

A little wine
on your birthday
is good for your heart.

A great big whine is
good for your attitude.

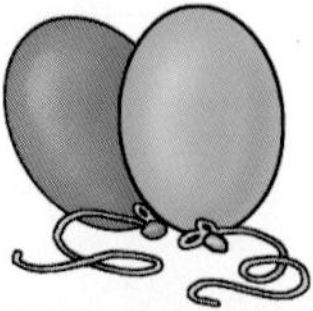

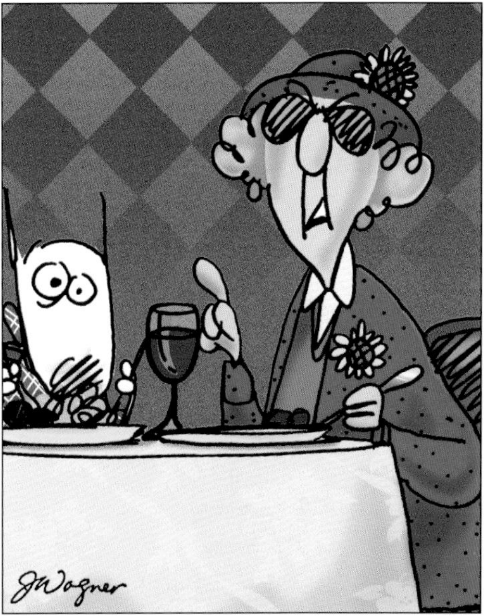
JWagner

Birthdays are a time when there's a whole lotta shakin' goin' on.

Yeah, those upper arms are always the first to go.

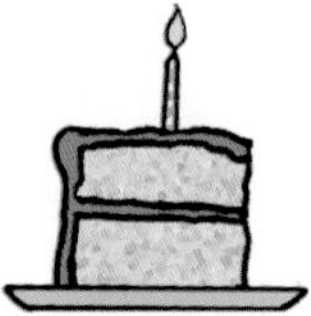

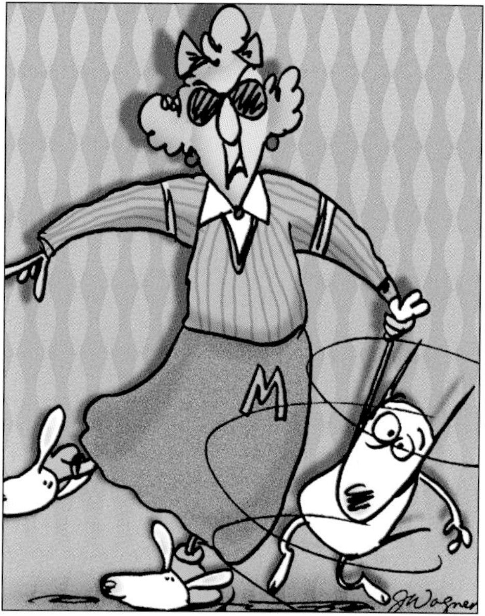
M
JWagner

When a birthday
invitation says
"bring a gag gift,"
I usually bring
a meatloaf.

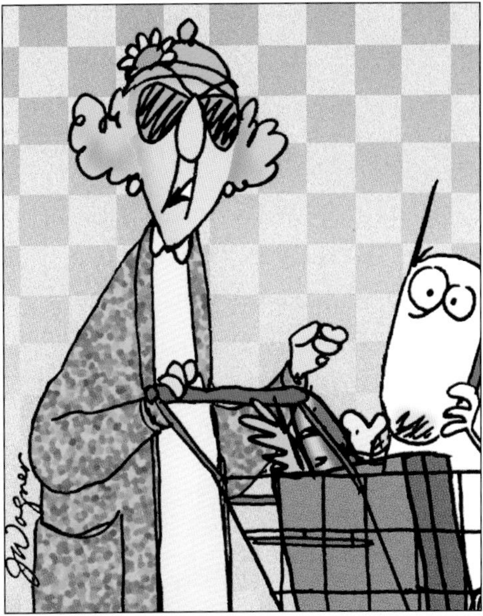
JWagner

Mother Nature
thinks of everything.

She makes your hair
turn gray before it
falls out so you don't
miss it as much.

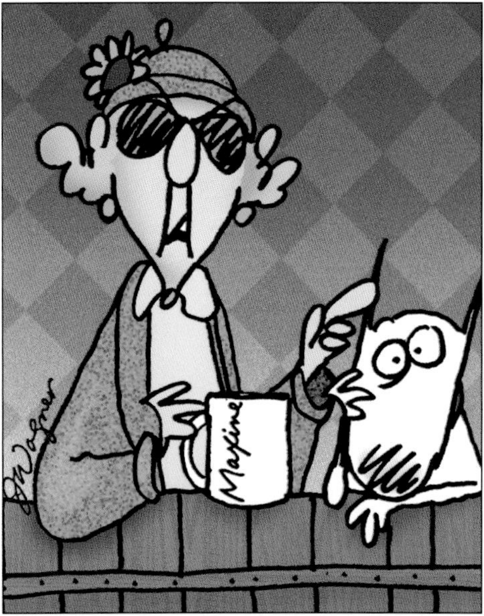
Maxine
Wagner

Some birthday gifts
just seem to say
"Open me first!"

While others cry
"Exchange me quickly!"

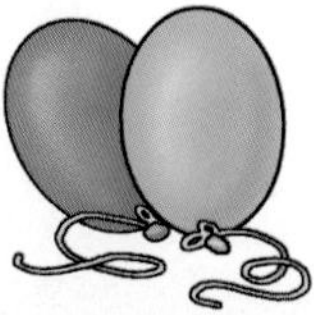

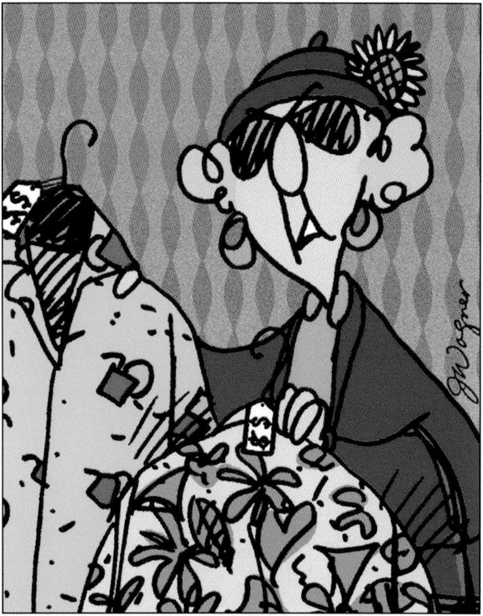

Birthdays are like
chocolate chip cookies.

If you think about
how many you've had,
it kinda makes you sick.

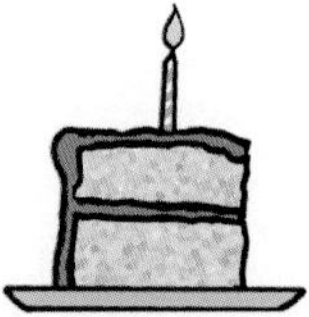

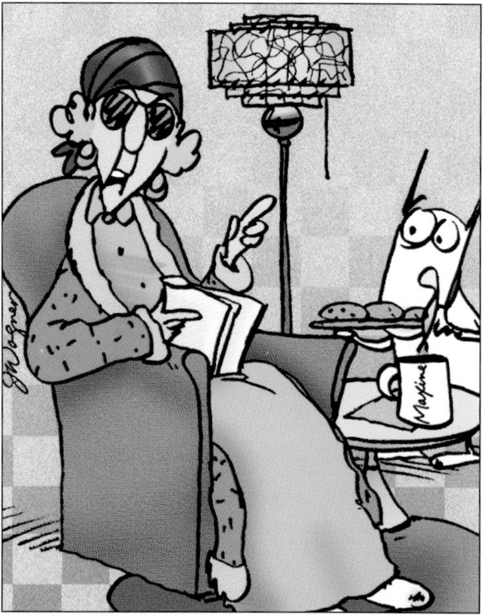
Maxine

Maxine

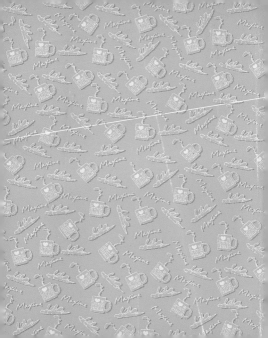